VOLUME 1

POEMS BY THE SPIRIT

BY

DARYL RICHARDSON

POEMS BY THE SPIRIT– VOLUME 1

COPYRIGHT 2001

PRINTED BY: BOOK LOGIX PUBLISHING SERVICES INC.

COVER DESIGN: GRAPHIC ARTIST MICHAEL HUNTER
PHOTO OF: THE LAST JUDGEMENT BY HANS MEMLING

HEAD SHOT BY: VANITY FAIR

ISBN #: 0-9710292-0-2

LIBRARY OF CONGRESS CONTROL #: 2001118959

UNLESS OTHERWISE NOTED SCRIPTURE QUOTATIONS ARE TAKEN FROM THE KING JAMES VERSION OF THE WORD OF GOD.

CONTENTS

ACKNOWLEDGEMENTS

IN MEMORY OF

DEDICATION

PREFACE

POEMS BY THE SPIRIT

ACKNOWLEDGEMENTS

I would first like to give Honor and Glory to my Lord and Savior Jesus Christ who enables me to do all things. I'd like to thank my family, friends and colleagues for your continual love and support.

I praise God for "The Prayer Group" and the Covenant that He Ordained. Our assignment is not over!

I must also recognize my former and present Pastors and the Anointed men and women of God who have had great impact and influence in my life.

Bishop Charles E Blake and First Lady Mae Blake
Pastors Floyd and Rev Elaine Flake
The Allen Liturgical Dance Ministry
Pastor A.R Bernard
Bishop TD Jakes
Prophetess Juanita Bynum
Dr. Cindy Trimm
Lance Walnau
Chuck Pierce
Dutch Sheets
Dr. Todd Coontz
Dr. Mike Murdock

IN MEMORY OF

My Loving Parents

Essie Lee Richardson   Fred Wilbur Richardson

1923-2001   1918-2006

You will always be
Forever with me
For I am your off-spring
And an extension of thee

My Dearest Brother

Donald Carey Richardson
1950-2006

You are my Hero

Your last choice in life extended ours

DEDICATION

Dedicated to my daughter Trinity whom I love more than words can express. Watching her grow and knowing that I am accountable to train her up in the way of the Lord is my greatest assignment and deepest joy. She will be all that God has called her too!

To all the children that I have had the privilege to come into contact with through teaching, I pray that you will walk in God's purpose for your life!

PREFACE

Why Poems by the Spirit?

This book came as a result of personal experiences and encounters in life. I always had the ability to write, but it wasn't until January of 1997 , that I realized that everything I do must Glorify God. It was May of that year that God began to anoint my writing.

Each poem is filled with the word of God and some reveal things that most people don't want to expose about themselves, but I now know that everything I have gone through has enabled me to help someone else. You can have influence on people when you have had the experience. I can share these unmentionables because I have overcome by the Blood of the Lamb (Jesus) and the word of my testimony. (Revelations 12:11)

I can no longer be under any condemnation for the choices I made prior to knowing the Lord and being pardoned from my sins. Who the Son sets free is free in deed!

The purpose of this book is to open your spiritual eyes a little wider in order for you to experience God a little deeper and receive continual revelation which is your life support. It is crucial that our mind is renewed daily whereby effecting our character and personality which will cause us to live a full victorious life in Christ Jesus.

In addition you will be informed of your adversary, the devil and the strategy he uses to deceive humanity. The Bible says in Ephesians 4:12 that we wrestle not against flesh and blood but against principalities, against powers, against the rulers of the darkness of this world, against spiritual wickedness in high places. God does not want us to be ignorant to the devil's devices. (II Corinthians 2:11)

Therefore as you go forth and partake of each poem, please ask God to search your heart so you can become aware of the things in your life that are keeping your from Him. This will enable you to examine yourself and make choices in life that are pleasing to God.

Please know that there is a fruitful garden within all of us, so let us pluck up the dead weeds so we can grow.

MY PRAYER

My prayer is that this book
will bare witness to your soul
And give you revelation
to complete and make you whole

To see into the spirit realm
what God has called you too
For many are in darkness
and don't even have a clue

of principalities and strongholds
and religious spirits too
You see Satan comes to church
and sometimes sits right next to you

To keep you from the fullness
and the walk God has ordained
Because yesterday, today and forever
Our God remains the same

We war against the flesh
that the mind and emotions lead
so I thank God in advance
for the planting of this seed

**Be Sober, be vigilant: Because your adversary the
devil, as a roaring lion, walketh about seeking whom
he may devour. (1Peter 5:8)**

GOD ORDAINED OR FLESH & BLOOD

A man shall leave his parents
And to his wife he'll cleave
What God has joined together
Is apparent your not to leave

But there is a discrepancy
Let's talk about divorce
Did God ordain the marriage
Or was it flesh & blood enforced?

I know a woman in the Lord
And four times married too
But those decisions she had made
Before God made her new

So now she's seeking Jesus
But to reach her husband is so hard
She's praying for his salvation
So he too can trust in God

It did not come to pass as yet
But of course she would endure
So she went to church and read her word
But he abused her more and more

With words that pierced her very soul
And caused the wounds within
My prayer was "God please change his heart
And turn him from his sin

Husbands should be head of their wives
As Christ is Head of the church
But he did not know Jesus
So their situation just got worse

Husbands are to love their wives
As Christ has loved the church
These scriptures must abide in marriage
In order to make it work

But then one night on Holy Ground
Within the midst of prayer
I said to God "Change his heart and mind
Or remove him out of there

Concerning unbelievers
If they leave let them depart
My prayer was answered one day later
Now God can mend her heart

Be not unequally yoked
With those who do not believe
That's an invitation to the devil
To pervert confuse and deceive

My heart cries out for marriages
That end up in divorce
But did God ordain the marriage
Or was it flesh & blood enforced

And many have experienced
Exactly what you've read
But put God first in all you do
And seek council before you wed

And even though it's in the past
And you said "it's now too late"
All things have become new in Christ
So seek God and don't speculate

For there is no condemnation
To those who are in Christ
Through Him you have salvation
He is the Way, the Truth and the Light

**And we know all things work together for good to
them that love God, to them who are called according
to His Purpose. (Romans 8:28)**

THE FRUIT OF THE SPIRIT

Patience is a virtue
Meaning not only for you to wait
But in doing so your demeanor
Must positively demonstrate

The Attributes of God
Described in Galatians 5:22
It's the very Fruit of the Spirit
That must exude and flow through you

The Love of God, His Joy and peace,
Long Suffering and being Kind
Goodness, Faithfulness, Gentleness
And Self-Control must be on your mind

Because those who are in Christ
Must crucify their flesh
And walk being led by the Spirit
And settle for nothing less

It's a level of maturity
To become more and more like Christ
However it is a conscious choice
And it will transform your very life

It's a place that God
Is calling us too
It's not by osmosis
But something you do

It's saying "Yes to the Lord'
This is a choice that I make
I want to abide in your shadow
While dwelling in your secret place

**He who dwelleth in the secret place of the Most High
God will abide under the shadow of the Almighty.
(Psalms 91:1)**

THE TERMS

God gives you the spirit of power
Not fear, but love and a sound mind
It's the intention God had from the beginning
After creating the Heaven, the Earth and mankind
The same Power God used in creation
He spoke things into manifestation
And now being the children of God
We can stand on that rooted foundation

God's plan caused our current existence
The never changing God is always consistent
That's why confession is made unto salvation
The words we speak are our life's affirmation
You see God walked in the garden with Adam
And sought fellowship in the cool of the day
All dominion and power was given
And the terms was just to obey

Those terms still apply in our life
We are under God's Grace through Jesus Christ
But our purpose in life can be put on delay
If we don't turn from our sins and begin to obey
So remember all power is given to thee
And great signs will follow them that believe

And in every deed for this cause, I have raised thee up to show in thee power. And that my name may be declared throughout all the earth. (Exodus 9:16)

YOUR WALK

Just to say the sinners prayer
Is simply not enough
You think your life will be easier
I promise you its tough

But through all the fiery darts
And blatant persecution
Just trust and rely in Jesus Christ
You know He is the world's solution

With all the tribulation
And problems that you face
Just count it all joy as you go through
And He will take you to that place

Of peace, love and assurance
Into your life He'll bring
The faith needed for endurance
In Jesus Christ our King

These things I have spoke to you, that in me ye might have peace. In the world ye shall have tribulation: But be of good cheer; I have overcome the world. (John 16:33)

AN AWESOME GOD

The earth is God's Footstool and Heaven is His Throne
If you ask Him for bread, will He in turn give you a stone?

God is to you, If you would only believe,
Your very life restitution, but its deliverance you need!

It may seem impossible to be completely understood
But as you seek and trust in God You'll come to know that
He is Good

You can't receive God with your intellect
The very conclusion you analyze will negate what
you expect

You see God's ways and thoughts are unreachable
But it's the spirit within you that is teachable

By prayer, supplication and seeking His Face
Will bring sufficiency in life which is found in His Grace

**How Awesome is the Lord Most High, the Great King
over all the Earth! (Psalms 47:2 NIV)**

TRUST IN THE LORD

Trust in God everyday
And He will bring you through
To be anxious for nothing
Is what His Word says not to do

So on in life we go,
Taking one day at a time
And Keeping your eyes on Jesus
You won't have time to look behind

He's the Way, the Truth and the Life
So please receive Him as such.
Because God gave his only begotten Son,
For this world that He loved so much

By prayer, supplication and thanksgiving,
God 's Word says: "let your requests be known".
Because the Children of God have access
To come boldly before God's Throne

I pray these words of promise
Will reach the depth of your being
It's the infallible word of God
And His Glory on Earth you'll be seeing

In the children who walk in obedience
That's what we are instructed to do
So God's Hand can be expedient
To ordain All that He has for you

Sometimes it so hard to imagine
something many can not perceive
But without Faith its impossible to please God
And its His Word you must stand on and believe

Distraction and opposition will come
In everything that you must endure
But rise above what you see and trust God
For your outcome is victorious for sure

**Remember ye not the former things, neither consider
the things of old. Behold I will do a new thing; Now it
shall spring forth; shall ye not know it? I will even
make a way in the wilderness, and rivers in the
desert. (Isaiah 43:19)**

Who You Are In Christ

Almighty God is watching us
from His Heavenly Throne
And we are Ambassadors for Christ on Earth
But never left alone

You must become aware
of God's Authority
It's the Power Jesus talks about
That is available for you and me

It's in the name of Jesus
That gives us all this right
But only if you made Him Lord
And the Savior of your life

And then you'll be drawn to Praise Him
And know you are a child of the King
And for those who walk uprightly
He will withhold no good thing

**For you are complete in Christ, which is the head of
all principality and power. (Colossians 2:10)**

I AM WHO I AM

I AM Jehovah Elyon,
The Living God, Most High
Heaven is my dwelling place
Above the clouds and sky

I AM Jehovah Jireh
Your Provision I will be
I own the cattle on a thousand hills
And the wealth of all eternity

I AM Jehovah Shamma,
I AM always right there
I AM Your Omnipotent Father
I AM also everywhere

I AM Jehovah Mequaddeshkem,
Which means I will sanctify
But it's your former ways and mindset
that you must crucify

I AM also your Shepherd
known as Jehovah Roi
Just seek my face in worship
And in my presence there is endless Joy

I AM Jehovah Ropheka,
I AM the God who heals
Just have faith and believe
And not in what you feel

I AM Jehovah Shalom,
And your peace I will always be
I'll take away every fear
And then set you free

I AM Jehovah Saboath
I AM your God of Hosts
I will lift every burden
And destroy every yoke

I Am Jehovah Nissi
And Jehovah Tsidkenu
I AM your banner and righteousness
And I will never leave or forsake you

**Be still and know that I AM God; I will be exalted
among the nations, I will be exalted in the earth.
(Psalms 46:10)**

Woman to Women

The existence of women
Was a needed creation
We are the recipient of life
With a nurturing foundation

The qualities we possess
Are truly from above
And the compassion we express
Can be filled with so much love

Our focus is usually directed
sometimes in the wrong place
When we're looking for a relationship
or perhaps a warm embrace

A man who finds a wife
Has truly found a good thing
So allow God to prepare us
For the husband He will bring

To sweep us off our feet
You know we all have had that dream
The man who has surrendered to God
Will treat you like a Queen

You see God knows what you desire
And He certainly knows what's best
So enjoy your time of singleness
And God will conquer that quest

Some men that you have chosen
Were disappointing and broke your heart
So consider it a Blessing
That you're currently apart

So ladies don't be discouraged
For we have all been going through
These words are meant to encourage
Now let Jesus fill that void in you!

My soul wait thou only upon God; for my expectation is from Him. (Psalms 62:5)

Woman to Men

I realize there's much pressure
In this world you face today
So why must you resist a God
That has prepared a way

The image that the world set up
Is not the truth at all
Because God has set a standard
And without it you will fall

You were God's first creation
And how pleased He was with you
But has God been invited
In all you choose to do

But it's all within a choice
And everyone must make their own
But if you pursue life without God
His Purpose for you won't be known

You see, when God is not the head of your life
and you've not surrendered your entire will
The devil thinks that he has a right
And your battle will be all up hill

The Lord God is seeking a yielding heart
To lead guide and protect
You do your part And Almighty God
Will ordain, manifest and direct

A word for men throughout every nation
God has set your destiny in motion
We are now in a new dispensation
Expect blessings like the waves in the ocean

So examine your heart
And take a stand
Reject the spirit of pride
To reach your promised land

Beware that thou forget not the Lord thy God in not keeping his statutes, which I commanded thee this day. (Deuteronomy 8:11)

BE ENCOURAGED

God has marvelous things for us
That we have yet to see
But Revelation comes from God
As we seek Him diligently

You see God will empower us
Like no one has ever seen
It's beyond man's wisdom
His visions and his dreams

Eye has not seen nor ear has not heard
What God has prepared
For it's written in His Word

Just know that God will prove Himself
Through your very situation
And prepare a table before your enemies
To complete His demonstration

So in the midst of your affliction,
Your trial and your test
Know that God will never leave you
And He's there to produce His best

**For I know the plans I have for you says the Lord.
They are plans for good and not for evil, to give you a
future and a hope. (Jeremiah 29:11) The Living Bible**

ABSTINENCE

To abstain from having sex
Is not the beginning of the end
You present your body to God
Then you begin to comprehend

The plans God has ordained
From the beginning of your life
Was for every woman to have a husband
And every man to have a wife

Another woman that I know
Whose blinders had been removed
She had a Revelation of all her choices
And knew God had disapproved

She asked God for His Forgiveness
And His Tender New Mercies too
It was His Power He bestowed upon her
That began to make her new

She made a re-commitment
Of her life to Christ again
To make a conscious choice in life
That she must not entertain sin!

She originally got saved
About 13 years ago
But she walked in disobedience
And the truth led her to know

That all that she pursued in life
And 5 abortions later
Made her finally realize
That she was a murderer and a fornicator

So she made a vow unto the Lord
"No more abortions" For it was slaughter
Then her Heavenly Father Blessed her
With a 7 lb. baby daughter

Her Dad was still around
And how she adored him so
But marriage was not a direction
That he was willing to go

So depending on the lust factor
He would come over and spend the night
She justified, he was her Dad
It was fine and he had a right

But she continued seeking God
And one day the Lord spoke to her
God said, "WILL YOU CONTINUE IN SIN?

She said NO! And He set her free

That is why I say to run from sex sin. No other sin af-
fects the body as this one does. When you sin this sin
it is against your own body. Haven't you learned that
your body is the home of the Holy Spirit God gave
you and He lives within you? Your own body does not
belong to you. For your body was bought with a great
price. So use every part of your body to give Glory
back to God. Because He owns it.
(1 Corinthians 6:18-20) Amplified Bible

DELIVERANCE

Deliverance is vital
But many are not aware
That the pulling down of strongholds
Is spiritual warfare

Take a good look at yourself
And don't deny all that you see
Only then can change take place
And that process will set you free

But only if your willing
And open to see the truth
Because we all have acquired habits
That we had engaged in since our youth

Question:

1. Are you walking the same walk when amidst a situation?

2. Are you talking the same talk when you seem
to feel frustration?

3. Is it a spirit of lies and elaboration that slips out?

4. Or is your attitude on the rise and your intention is to
pout?

The Answer

These things ought not to be
Resist your flesh and those thoughts will flee
Submit to God and desire His Traits
Because God's path to righteousness is Narrow and straight

Cast down vain imaginations
And everything that comes to mind
Based on your emotions
And life you said you left behind!

Finally be strong in the Lord and in His mighty power, Put on the whole armor of God so that you can stand against the devil's schemes. For our struggle is not against flesh and blood but against rulers, against the authorities, against the powers of this dark world and against spiritual forces of evil in the Heavenly realms. (Ephesians 6:10-12) NIV Bible

TAKING A MOMENT

Many times we're running here and there
And nothing is getting done
We think we must be productive
So we're constantly on the run

And all that we attempt to do
Is sometimes just so hard
That's why it's so important
To be still and trust in God

But often we engage in things
That are easy for us to do
They are usually distractions
From what God has called us too

So be still and take a moment
And cultivate your ear
Because God is always talking
And He so wants you to hear

**But they that wait on the Lord shall renew their strength;
They shall mount up like wings as eagles; they shall run
and not be weary; they shall walk, and not faint.
(Isaiah 40:31)**

MY CONFESSION

I am blessed and highly favored
And prospering in wealth
I claim all that God has promised
And I'm walking in perfect health

The visions God has shown me
I will do my part thus far
Then begin to call those things
That be not as though they are

According to His riches
God supplies all of my needs
The Glory of God is upon me
To cause me to succeed

You see I know whom I belong too
I'm the head and not the tail
No weapon formed against me
And the gates of hell shall not prevail

I walk in the Favor of God
With all Wisdom, Knowledge and Glory
I'm above and not beneath
For His Promises are my story!

This book of the law shall not depart from your mouth, but meditate on it day and night, that you may observe to do according to all that is written in it. For then you will make your way prosperous and then you will have good success. (Joshua 1:8)

WORDS

The words from your mouth
must be positive confession
They must line up with the word of God
To receive your promised possession

The words that you speak
can go forth in one's life
Are they words spoken in Love
or are they stirring up strife

It is written in the scriptures
That the tongue can no man tame
When negative thoughts enter your mind
Just rebuke them and refrain

From causing them to enter
Into the atmosphere
You see God above is listening
And Satan too can hear

The Bible says we wrestle
Not against flesh and blood
But principalities and power
in the spirit realm above

So eat live and receive God's Word
It's manna in this very hour
Because God through Christ
has given us All Dominion, Authority and Power

Over every single creeping thing
In the sea and in the air
So let's walk in all God says we are
Binding up spiritual warfare

Therewith bless we God, even the Father; and therewith curse we men which are made after the similitude of God. Out of the same mouth proceedeth blessing and cursing. My brethren these things ought not to be. (James 3:9-10)

TONGUES

The Holy Ghost that we can receive
Falls upon us from God on high
It's the evidence of speaking in tongues
And we certainly must not pass it by

For that is the power of God
That is mentioned in Acts I and 8
Jesus gave instructions
And His Disciples did not hesitate

Anyone who will ask can receive
You must simply have faith and believe
But WOE unto the Pastor that is preaching
Against speaking in tongues and not teaching

Everything that is written in God's Word
For you will give an account, haven't you heard?

And these signs shall follow them that believe; In my name they shall cast out devils; they shall speak with new tongues. (Mark 16:17)

Q & A

PEOPLE SAY

People Say "The Word of God, I just don't understand Did God really write it, or was it written by man?

The Word of God "People Say" How can I believe? Is it merely just a fable or something I should receive

People Say "The Word of God, was it written long ago And now things are so different so how am I to know

If everything that's written is truly from above And who's this God they talk about that's filled with so much love?

GOD SAYS

The answers to your questions
Are spiritually discerned
It's something you believe
And not something that you learn

According to your mind
You will never comprehend
Because I AM revealed
Through the Spirit man within

31

Step one is to surrender
And yield your very soul
I promise you I'll show up
And begin to make you whole

For you all have a purpose
That I have designed
And it will be revealed
In my perfect Will and Time

Now the choice is up to you
And its Jesus you must choose
You'll have absolutely all to gain
And not a thing to loose

But your old ways and your thoughts
And your opinions, You ask why?
So your mind will be renewed
And your former ways must die

If you choose to accept my Son
And receive Him in your heart
You will then have eternal life
And on Earth a brand new start

So you now begin to ponder
And wonder if your life is ok
But once Jesus becomes your Savior
You will know He is the way

It's being born again
And everything will become new
My Word is here to instruct you
And a roadmap to what you should do

It's my Spirit that will teach you
And guide you as you go your way
It's beyond all of your comprehension
Just receive Christ in your heart today

Thus saith God the Lord, He that created the Heavens and stretched them out; He that spread forth the earth, and that which cometh out of it: He that giveth breath unto the people upon it, and Spirit to them that walketh therein; I the Lord have called thee in righteousness and will hold thine hand and will keep thee. (Isaiah 42:5-6)

THE BEST MAN– 2001

I know a man who's 35
But at times I think he's 10
He's a man of God who loves the Lord
And he says that he's born again

But the Bible says a tree is judged
By all of it's good fruit
Is he hiding behind his Mercedes Benz
His good looks and his suit?

But all these things shall pass away
And God will judge his heart
Is he being all that God is calling him too?
Or is he afraid to yield and do his part

All of these things
God has allowed me to see
But the question I have
Is what keeps drawing me?

Am I desiring this man,
Is He God's choice for my life?
You see God knows I've been praying
To become someone's wife

Does he see me as
God says I am?
God's Diamond, His Jewel,
His most precious Gem

I pray for this man
And intercede as well
But the final conclusion
Is only time will tell

The one thing that I've learned
Is to pull back and don't push
If he does not step up to the plate
God has a ram in the bush

9 years later
he has come around
Said he encountered God
But was still lost and not found

Still stuck in a mind set
Based on the things of this world
He says "he desires to marry
But is still looking for the right girl

Sometimes what we are looking for
Is right before our eyes
But if we don't know who we are
The very thing we will despise

You see the natural eyes are blinded
When one's life is not surrendered
Then God's Plan and Purpose for our lives
Will ultimately be hindered

To know your future and destiny
Can only be revealed
When Jesus Christ is truly Lord
Don't Stop...Don't Go....Just Yield!

As the Lord God said, it is not good that man should be alone; I will make him a helper compatible to him. (Genesis 2:18)

BODY, SOUL & SPIRIT

The flesh that covers our body
Is over our spirit and soul
But seeking God diligently
Is what begins to make us whole

This body is a shell
That one day goes back to the dust
This flesh that we respond too
In it's passions and it's lust

The soul that is mistaken
For the spirit man with in
And then we find ourselves
Within uncompromising sin

The spirit of a person
Is in the deeper inner parts
It's the living spirit of God
And its closer to your heart

Created in God's Image
It's the spirit He's referring too
To put the flesh under subjection
Is the part that we must do

It's a daily conscious effort
And we must draw nigh to God
Because this flesh was born in iniquity
And makes spending time with Him so hard

But press to receive His hidden treasures
It's Revelation from seeking His face
The necessity to walk in the fullness of God
And he will reveal your Purpose and place

There are many that don't
Really understand
That the weapons of our warfare
Are in such a great demand

And God has put all authority within our very hand

**So they that are in the flesh cannot please God.
(Romans 8:8)**

HOW DO I KNOW

How do I know when it's you Lord
And how can I be totally sure
God said when I begin to reason
Its something I should ignore

How do I know when it's you Lord
If it's you that I actually hear
I praise and worship and enter into your presence
Than I diligently seek you in prayer

How do I know when its you Lord
Your Word says "Your sheep know your voice'
I keep my eyes fixed on Jesus
And in Him I will always rejoice

How do I know when it's you Lord
I must keep my mind stayed on thee
Don't look to the left or the right
And don't be moved by anything I see

I now know, that I know, when it's you Lord
I surrender, submit and endure
I know who I AM now in Christ
And by Faith I can totally be sure

That the God of Heaven
Is Faithful and Just
And His Word
You can depend on and trust

**Trust in the Lord with all thine heart; and lean not to your own understanding. In all thy ways acknowledge Him and He will direct thy paths.
(Proverbs 3:5-6)**

WICKED GENERATION

Fire and Brimstone and gnashing of teeth
Describes the lake of Fire
And it shall not cease
In a twinkle of an eye,
The Lord Jesus shall return
And those who have rejected Him,
Will end of their and burn
Fornication, Adultery and Homosexuality today
You must resist that way of life
And seek deliverance as you pray
Satisfying your flesh and the spirit of lust
The Word of God is the answer
And His mandate you must trust
You can be set free and delivered
But you must renew your mind
Sanctification and Holiness
Will come in a matter of time
This Wicked generation
That the devil has ruled
Attacking our youth
And taking prayer out of school

A DECISION SUCH AS THAT WAS MADE BY A FOOL!

But every knee shall bow
And it's Jesus you will confess
So receive Him, Pray and read your word
Then witness to all the rest

**Yet if thou warn the wicked, and he turn not from his
wickedness nor from his wicked way, he shall die in
his iniquity; but thou has delivered thy soul.
(Ezekiel 3:19)**

IDOL WORSHIP

Idol worship is a sin
or did you even know
So begin to search your life
To discover those things that have to go

Is it watching television
Where you spend most of your time
Or a man or woman in your life
That you think is "Oh so fine"

Is it shopping that intrigues you
Designer clothes of a fancy car
Or spending time in acting class
To be Hollywood's next star

These are things you must inquire
And merely ask yourself
God says "Have no other god's before Him"
Absolutely nothing else

These things that are so important
Are they put before the Lord?
Because our God is a jealous God
And you simply can't afford

To continue on in life
Not recognizing what you've done

God must be your priority
He must be number one

So now that I have your attention
Please take this time to reflect

That wherever you apply your energy
Will have a lifetime effect

So keep your eyes on Jesus
You'll have more than you'll ever expect

Woe to my rebellious children says the lord; You ask advice from everyone but me, and decide to do what I don't want you to do. You yoke yourself with unbelievers, thus piling up your sins. (Isaiah 30:1)

NOT TO GIVE GLORY
JUST TELLING HIS STORY

Lucifer was a praise angel
That walked to and fro God's throne
Then pride entered his heart
And he wanted to reign on his own

To be exalted above God in the North
Where he was to dwell on high
No way in Heaven would God allow it
Give permission or even to comply

So God cast him out of Heaven
And the angels he deceived too
This was the devil's opportunity
To make his earthly debut

Sin, sickness and disease in our Nation
Is definitely on the rise
Fornication, adultery and homosexuality
Is by no means a big surprise

Satan has taken God's Creation
To deceive and pervert a Nation

And those who live without Christ
Will end up in eternal damnation

You say "there couldn't be a place such as this"
Because you don't believe in the devil

But that's to keep you from the truth
And deceive you on his level

You see good and evil does exist
But we have a choice and we must resist

Because Satan is the master strategist
A deceiver and the father of lies

It was in the Garden of Eden
That he used a snake as his clever disguise

You see there is nothing new under the sun
And all the sin has already been done

It's repetition in it's awful state
And it appears that there's no way for escape

But there is a way and I know His Name
And one day this world will not be the same

And all you have to do is proclaim
Because Jesus will not make you ashamed

To live for Jesus is what you must desire
Because without Him your eternity is the lake of fire

And that great dragon was cast out, the old serpent called the devil, and Satan, which deceiveth the whole world; He was cast out into the earth, and all his angels were cast out with him. (Revelation 12:9)

IT'S YOUR CHOICE

Sin in an eternal cancer
We're not aware of how it can spread

We must turn from our ways to please God
And walk forth in our blessings ahead

It's an unruly evil within us
When we live our life fulfilling the flesh

A carnal mind is enmity with God
And the outcome of that life is death

Just as cancer can eat you alive
Sin will enable you not to survive

God is separating the wheat from the tares
He is making His Presence aware

So make a choice of whom you will serve
Because God hastens to perform His Word

**This day I call heaven and earth as witnesses against
you that I have set before you life and death, bless-
ing and cursing. Now choose life, so that you and
your children may live and that you may love the
Lord your God, listen to His voice and hold fast to
Him. For the Lord is your life and He will give you
many years in the land He swore to your Fathers,
Abraham, Isaac and Jacob. (Deuteronomy 30:19)
NIV Bible**

ONLY HUMAN

There's no cure for humanity
A man of God once said

That statement had an impact on my life
What light it shed

That people have personalities
and multiple character traits

All the reason God commands
And abhor from exhibiting hate

The flaws that we possess
May not ever seem to cease

But they will appear invisible
When we begin to walk in God's Peace

We must begin to see each other
As if we had God's eyes

And seek His characteristics
For this my friend is wise

It's His Grace that will enable you
To demonstrate the ways of God

When you do things by your own means
Is a struggle and seems so hard

It's about what God has ordained
And our purpose we must seek to obtain

We're here on earth to fulfill that plan
It's a desire He has for us all

Just say "Lord have your way in my life"
And He will respond to your call

**My Grace (My favor and loving-kindness and mercy)
is enough for you (sufficient against any danger and
enables you to bear the trouble manfully) For my
strength and power are made perfect (fulfilled and
completed) and show themselves most effective in
(your) weakness. (II Corinthians 12:9)
Amplified Bible**

WHAT TIME IT IS!

We're living on the edge
Of a Millennial switch
The transference of the wealth
Will make the righteous rich

To promote and expand God's kingdom
Right here on the earth
All of what God has called you too
Was established before your birth

God will unfold the Miracles
That is waiting to be released
No weapon formed against it
And every obstacle will cease

This season that we're in
God is pouring out His favor
Be focused and unmovable
And do not doubt or waver

The Bible says the wealth of the wicked
Is laid up for the just
Is your life pleasing to God
And are you someone He can trust

With what you have right now
Let you spending become wise
And I will tell you how
To enhance God's enterprise

Do not put your money
Into the hands of the wicked
But replenish it and plant
Within the Body of Christ

So God's Kingdom can be promoted
And put 1000 demons to flight

But seek God's instructions
On what soil to plant your seed
The ground must be fertile
To produce a great harvest indeed

**I make known the end from the beginning, from the
ancient times, what is still to come. I say: My pur-
pose will stand and I will do all that I please from the
east I summon a bird of prey; from the afar off land,
a man to fulfill my purpose. What I have said, that
will I bring about, what I have planned, that will I
do.(Isaiah 46:10-11) NIV Bible**

YOUR AUTHORITY

Have you commanded the morning
To cause the day to take its place
To get an advantage on Satan
Before he begins the race

God will orchestrate your footsteps
And give you favor throughout your day
Because our God desires to obligate
Himself in every way

As long as it's line with
What the Word of God has said
So your mind will be renewed
And your spirit will be fed

He delights in your praise and worship
They are melodic chimes to His Heavenly ear
And you will receive answers
when you seek the Lord in prayer

Everywhere you tread your feet
That is territory claimed
Taking Jesus into the market place
Is what God has ordained

And I have given you authority over all the power of the enemy, and to walk among serpents and scorpions and to crush them. Nothing shall injure you! However the important thing is not that the demons obey you, but that your names are registered as citizens of Heaven. (Luke 10:19-20) The Living Bible

IN CLOSING:

WHAT I HOPE FOR YOU

The human mind submits to what is familiar and conducive to one's life. My prayer is that you sincerely examine your life, your choices, your attitude and character and measure them by each poem and the Word of God. "Poems by the Spirit" is the Word of God in Poetry form. God wants to perfect the things that concern you and me, and we must be willing to realize that we need help. We all fall short of the Glory of God and if any of these poems bare witness with you, and you would like God to deal with those areas that you have not mastered simply confess the following prayer:

Lord God I know I have issues in my life that I have not been able to overcome. I want to first acknowledge that you loved me so much that you sent your Beloved Son Jesus to die on the cross for all of my sins, sickness and disease. Lord I ask if there is any un-forgiveness, bitterness, jealousy, envy or strife in my heart, reveal it so I can cast it out. Lord I desire an impartation of the fruit of the spirit so I can exemplify you publically and privately and be a living Epistle of Christ in the earth and walk in my divine purpose and anointing in my sphere of influence.

Future books awaiting God's timing of release are Volume 2 of "Poems by the Spirit" "Before the Fire & After the Flame" and the Phenomenal book "Miracles, Yesterday, Today and Forever"

"Miracles, Yesterday, Today and Forever" contain real life miracles and testimonies that individuals have shared. It will Bless, encourage and reaffirm what a Mighty God we serve.

If you would like to testify to what God has done in your life, please write and share it with me. Your experience can be published in a volume of Miracles, Yesterday, Today and Forever and witness to someone else. Always remember; We overcome by the blood of the lamb and the word of our testimony. (Revelation 12:11)

In addition to this book each poem is available in card form so you can witness to those unsaved individuals and loved ones.

Write to:
Poems by the Spirit
PO BOX 341449
Rochdale Village NY, 11434

www.ingramcontent.com/pod-product-compliance
Lightning Source LLC
Chambersburg PA
CBHW060200070426
42447CB00033B/2245